Xmas - 1990

BOOMERANG

Fr. Chester Wrzaszczak

Father Chester Wrzaszczak

Resource Publications, Inc.
160 E. Virginia St. #290
San Jose, CA 95112

Editorial director: Kenneth Guentert
Production editor: Elizabeth J. Asborno
Art director: Ron Niewald
Cover design: Andrew Wong
Cover production: Ron Niewald and Andrew Wong
Illustrations: George Collopy

Library of Congress Cataloging in Publication Data

Wrzaszczak, Chester Francis, 1917-
  Boomerang, and other Easter stories.

  Summary: A collection of stories describing a variety of Easter experiences.
  I. Title.
BV55.W7 1988   263'.93   88-30692
ISBN 0-89390-131-8

5 4 3 2 1
92 91 90 89 88

To all the children
and young people
at St. Anne Church,
Portland, Oregon
and at all the other parishes
I was priveleged to serve
in my forty-three years
as God's priest

Contents

Acknowledgments

We are deeply indebted to Charlotte Smalley, BA, for originally illustrating these stories and suggesting some of them.

We also owe a debt of gratitude to Sister Mary De Porres, C.S.S.F., MSW, who proofread and typed the manuscript.

We acknowledge them as doing this not only in this book but also in its predecessor, *St. Francis and the Christmas Miracle* (San Jose, CA: Resource Publications, 1986).

Most of all we acknowledge God as the Original Author for whom the undersigned served as a poor, priestly pen.

Father Chester Wrzaszczak, JCD, STL, BA.

To the Readers

Dearest Children—and Grown-Ups:

These ten stories are for your entertainment as well as enlightenment.

We hope you'll enjoy them and learn a little more about our Christian faith.

Most of all we pray, as you read, that you'll draw closer to God and our Blessed Mother and *love them more than ever before.*

Your author would be very pleased were this to happen.

So would God.

Love,

Father Chester Wrzaszczak (pronounced V-shah-sh-chock)
Retired Pastor of St. Anne Church
Portland, Oregon, Easter, 1988

P.S. The footnotes are to help you learn more new words! The pronunciation (pro-nun-see-a-shun) guide is the author's own.

Ethel's Easter Outfit

It happened every year—regularly.

Just before Easter, Ethel's two elderly aunts invited her to their home. The purpose was to treat Ethel to a hearty, wholesome dinner and to give her some used clothes for the coming holiday. It was sort of a ritual.[1] The two relatives were the sisters of Ethel's mom. They were fairly wealthy, whereas Ethel and her family were rather poor.

---

1. Rit-chew-el: a ceremony, usually done the same way every time.

Ethel waited impatiently all year for the visit. Her parents, unfortunately, did not visit the two aunts because of some misunderstanding years ago that made for a strained and tense relationship. In other words, the four adults just didn't get along.

So once a year during Holy Week, usually on Good Friday, Ethel would walk all by herself across town, a full two miles, to spend the day in the fine, well-furnished home owned by the two well-to-do women. They were twins, but one, Miriam, was a spinster.[2] Margaret was a widow[3] whose husband had died several years ago. Both were in their late sixties, of medium height, weight, and coloring: gray eyes and gray hair, but gentle and genial,[4] especially when company came over. The widow had to use a wheelchair most of the time. When she got out of her chair, she had to use a cane to get to the bathroom and bedroom.

Ethel was a beautiful twelve-year-old girl: bright, brown-eyed, a brunette with cute deep dimples, very thoughtful with a sensitive mouth but a determined, strong, square chin and full-blown lips. She was a devoted daughter and a devout, caring Christian who attended church weekly and helped others regularly. She loved books, read much, and studied diligently.[5] She hoped to be a surgeon[6] some day, not merely a physician like the one you see in the office when you're sick.

2. Spin-ster: an older, unmarried woman.
3. Wid-doe: a woman whose husband is dead.
4. Gee-nee-al: cheerful.
5. Dill-a-gently: constantly and with concentration.
6. Sir-gen: a doctor who operates on people.

Ethel's aunts encouraged her and helped her, at least once a year. Aunt Margaret would give Ethel her daughter's discarded[7] dresses—we call them "hand-me-downs."[8] The daughter attended a private boarding school and was seldom home. The spinster, Aunt Miriam, always gave Ethel a ten dollar check for personal use and school expenses. Ethel felt like an adult[9] when she went to the bank, endorsed[10] the check, and cashed it at the teller's window in the bank. She would watch the teller count out ten singles, crisp, new dollars, with disbelief[11] at such good fortune. The teller would always smile and say something like, "Don't lose it" or "Be sure to put it in your purse or pocket right away and keep your hand on it!"

Good Friday dinner at her aunts' house was also an unforgettable event. No meat was eaten, however. Since the Lord gave up His life on the cross for love of us on Good Friday, so we ought to give up meat out of love for Jesus on Good Friday. To make up for the absence of meat, Ethel's aunts had a surprising variety of other foods. As children aren't exactly excited about fish on Friday, the hostesses[12] prepared the most delicious dishes, such as dumplings served with drawn[13] butter, dozens of different homemade doughnuts fried in deep fat (Ethel still remembers the sizzling and can still smell the aroma[14]),

7. Dis-car-ded: cast off, thrown aside.
8. Originally, used clothing handed down from older to younger children; now meaning any used article one gets.
9. Ad-ult: a grown-up person.
10. En-dorse: sign one's name on the back of a check.
11. Dis-bee-leaf: unbelieving.
12. Host-ess-ses: women who *host* people by serving them food or inviting them to their homes as guests.
13. Drawn: melted.
14. A-rome-ah: fragrant odor.

dark bread with thick slabs of cheddar and swiss cheese, and oh yes, a cup of clear soup from a secret recipe. Topping it all was a pitcher of homemade root beer. Ethel could have had ice cream too, but for love of God said simply, "No, thank you. I'll offer it up to Jesus."

This year there was an unusual surprise awaiting Ethel. She didn't know a thing about it. The aunts gave no clues although they had talked about it for some time with each other. They decided that since Ethel would turn thirteen after Easter and become a teenager, she shouldn't be wearing hand-me-downs any longer. "She's such a darling girl and doesn't mind taking her cousin's clothes when she has outgrown them. But it's time to give her something *new* for a change! Even poor people like to receive, at least once in a while, an article that's not second-hand but brand new" was their consensus.[15]

Imagine Ethel's surprise when, after that delicious dinner and the clean up, her Aunt Miriam announced, "I have to go shopping downtown tonight for Easter. I'll take the crosstown trolley. Ethel dear, why don't you come along? From downtown you'll have only one mile to walk back home instead of two." Ethel was all smiles. She kissed Aunt Margaret on her cheery cheek and received her blessing[16] as was the family custom. She didn't see her wink at Aunt Miriam, which signalled they were still keeping their secret from Ethel. As she was leaving, Ethel felt some disappointment that Aunt Margaret did not invite her upstairs as usual to help herself to some of her

---

15. Kon-sen-sus: agreement.
16. A prayer or sign of the cross for God's goodness or grace.

cousin's discarded dresses, shoes, stockings, and sweaters. Both her aunts seemed to have forgotten, so Ethel said nothing.

When the trolley car rattled and rocked into the downtown area, Aunt Miriam took Ethel by the arm and asked sweetly, "Do you mind shopping with me, child? You have time. It's only 6:30."

Ethel was startled but pleased by the unusual and unexpected invitation. She felt proud, pleased, important enough for her aunt to choose her as a shopping companion.

The two turned down Davis Drive, then strolled over to the wide windows of Wilson's Women's Dress Shop on Walker Way.

Such lovely dresses on those tall, slender manikins,[17] and such darling outfits for teenaged girls! Shiny shoes and silk stockings (nylons hadn't been invented then) were also on display.

"Let's do our shopping here," Aunt Miriam declared after studying the pieces. Ethel has never seen such beautiful and expensive articles of wear in her whole life.

Then came the next surprise.

The salesperson was told, "Outfit this girl for Easter."

Ethel almost fainted.

Flushed with excitement, but feeling this was too much for her aunt to do, she stammered, "Auntie, you don't have to..."

---

17. Man-nick-kins: store "dummies," life-like models or figures of people made of cardboard, wood, wire, plastic.

"Yes I do have to. You are my only niece and soon to be a teenager. This Sunday you can join the Easter Parade[18] as so many other people do."

Ethel did not join any parade.

She wore her new outfit to church on Easter morning so as to honor Christ on His Resurrection,[19] to express her joy that He came back to life out of love for us just as He had died on the cross for love of us.

Because of the kindness shown Ethel by her gracious aunts, Ethel's parents apologized to them. They all kissed and made up. Peace was restored and a loving relationship was resumed[20] between the relatives, once they had been reconciled.[21]

Ethel was unable to become that surgeon she dreamed about. However, she did become an artist. To this day she paints and sculpts[22] and remembers her twelfth Easter Sunday!

18. Easter parades probably come from the early Christian days when those who were to be baptized, (see footnote 18a) called catechumens (see footnote 18b), were given new, white linen garments to wear after being baptized. They wore them all through Easter week. Soon their family and friends wore new clothes as they joined the catechumens. Later people began to parade around town, even out into the fresh spring meadows, in their Easter finery, especially for Sunrise Service on early Easter morning. Years ago in New York City, thousands of people dressed in new clothes and Easter bonnets (not Easter bunnies!) and paraded down Fifth Avenue in what became known as the Annual Easter Parade. It was eventually copied by people everywhere!

18a. Bap-tize-d: made Christians by a religious ceremony called the Sacrament of Baptism.

18b. Cat-teh-cue-mens: people who had been catechized (cat-teh-kized); that is, instructed and prepared for Baptism.

19. Res-sur-reck-shun: to "arise again"; that is, become alive again.

20. Re-soomed: started again.

21. Rec-kon-siled: united after being forgiven and after forgiving.

22. Skull-pts: makes clay figures and "fires" them in a kiln till they get hard and durable (dur-a-bull).

The Easter Basket

Ciesiu[1] was a server, an altar boy.

How he enjoyed to hurry over to church from his humble home across the street and through the schoolyard every morning! He regarded "serving Mass," as it was then described, as a great privilege and a pleasure. Because of this loving and lovable attitude and because he lived so close to the parish church, he served often. Sometimes the other servers would miss their turn, especially in very cold, snowy, or rainy weather. When this happened, Mr. Kozak,

1. Cheh-shoo: Polish for "little Chester of Ceslaus (Sess-loss)."

the caretaker, wouldn't ring the church bells on schedule. This was a secret signal for Ciesiu to hasten over from his house and act as a substitute server. The caretaker would then ring the bells, which awakened the entire neighborhood. However, people in those days didn't mind because very few had alarm clocks to awaken them. They were poor, immigrant Polish people who couldn't afford clocks, although some did have quaint European wall clocks.[2]

Well, not only were Ciesiu's parents as poor as nearly all their fellow Poles in America and elsewhere, but worse. At this time in Ciesiu's life, his father was laid off from work at the freight yards on Western Avenue. His mother found part-time employment as a char woman (that is, sweeping and scrubbing floors at night in Chicago's downtown office buildings and big department stores). Many other mothers had to do this kind of work to earn money for food for the family. Unfortunately, just as Lent, the season before Easter, was about to begin, Ciesiu's mother was also laid off work. It was that dreadful Depression, when millions of people around the world were unemployed and living in poverty.

Now, Lent is a time for great numbers of religious folk everywhere to do something special for

---

2. These were the old-fashioned kind with a swinging pendulum (see footnote 2a) that they had brought with them from "the old country." Those clocks had no alarms, but they struck every hour on the hour day and night. Sound sleepers like Ciesiu never heard the twelve chimes strike every midnight, but they did hear those same twelve chimes at noon because noontime is twelve o'clock p.m.

2a. Pend-jew-loom

God and others: a "penance," like praying more frequently and more fervently, helping others worse off than you are, visiting the sick, running errands for the elderly, etc. One was also expected to improve himself or herself, too. Getting rid of bad habits such as laziness, disobedience, lack of love and sensitivity for others' feelings—in other words, becoming a better Christian—was the way to spend the Lenten season. It was also the custom, and still is, to forego certain foods on Fridays, especially meat, and for adults to eat less often and take smaller amounts of food at their meals. Foregoing meat on Fridays is called "abstinence;" eating less food is known as "fasting."

During Lent in the year 1930, Ciesiu and his family never saw meat at all except on Sundays—and they fasted almost daily simply because there wasn't enough to eat. Nobody knew this as the family never told anyone. "Everybody has to go hungry sooner or later," Ciesiu's dad would say sorrowfully. "We will offer up our hunger to Jesus, who went hungry forty days and forty nights in the *pustynia*,[3] and even before that when He was a boy. The Holy Family was poor too." Such words encouraged Ciesiu to keep his chin up and his eyes down when passing a bakery, a fruitstand, or a candy store. These were found even in the middle of the block in many ethnic[4] areas where immigrants from foreign countries settled.

3. Poo-stin-yah: Polish for "desert, wilderness."
4. Eth-nick: of foreign origin or nation.

That Lent, therefore, passed slowly for Ciesiu, but soon it was Holy Week, the last seven days before Easter Sunday. So many moving, inspiring services almost every evening in church! The boy was asked to assist at all of them. Father Rahshock, the round, robust pastor of Five Polish Martyrs Church, knew his server would never miss a practice session for each service—and he always did his part so beautifully and reverently. Sister Sylvestra also depended on him. Sister was a sacristan.[5] Ciesiu would help set up the articles necessary for Mass while his cousin, Kinga, would aid Sister in arranging the flowers. Such activities helped Ciesiu forget his hunger pains. Tall Sister Sylvestra and tiny Kinga never noticed this.

After the sad and sorrowful Good Friday ceremonies, Ciesiu couldn't wait for Holy Saturday afternoon. What was so special about Holy Saturday afternoon? Well, in many ethnic churches, especially the Polish ones, there was a wonderful tradition, an ancient custom of bringing beautifully decorated baskets full of Easter food to be blessed by the priest. Ciesiu would stand at the priest's side, holding a holy water sprinkler for as many as six blessings, every hour on the hour beginning at 1 p.m. and ending at 6 p.m.

Oh, the aroma of those blest and even unblest Polish goodies! Almost all the baskets contained a baked ham encircled by a rich ring of succulent Polish sausage called *kielbasa*[6]; a fragrant fresh loaf

5. Sak-ri-sten: someone in charge of the sacred vessels, vestments, etc., that the priest uses in the sanctuary and at the altar.
6. Kel-bah-sah: a smoked or unsmoked Polish sausage.

of Polish rye bread with a cross traced on top as a reminder of Christ crucified[7]; a cake shaped like a lamb with frosting that resembled the white, woolly coat of a sheep (Jesus is also the Lamb of God). There was another lamb, one made out of butter with pepper seeds for eyes and a red ribbon around its neck as on the cake lamb. Tucked in corners were tiny jars of salt and horseradish, and lining the sides of the basket were hard-boiled eggs painted with the most gorgeous colors and intricate[8] designs. Parents or older children carried the baskets, their delicious aromatic contents covered with pretty, hand-sewn, artistically stitched linen and cotton cloths. Smaller children often carried their own cute little baskets filled mostly with marshmallow eggs, candy lambs, chocolate bunnies, and of course, jelly beans, to remind us that Easter is the season of spring and the new life Jesus brought to us by coming back to life after his death on Good Friday.

Ciesiu's mouth watered as he faced with Father Rahshock these many, many baskets awaiting the priest's blessing. He had to keep back his tears. No one this year would come from his family with a basket. They couldn't afford it. The aroma of the food was becoming stronger by the hour as people came and went. By the time the fifth group of basket bearers began to assemble in church for the blessing of their Easter goodies, Ciesiu felt a little dizzy. At the sixth and final blessing, as he was about to hand Father the holy water sprinkler at the end of the

7. Crew-si-fied: nailed to a cross.
8. In-trick-ate: complicated.

priest's prayer over the food, Ciesiu blacked out. He dropped the brass sprinkler, swayed, then slowly slid to the floor.

He lay in a dead faint.

No one moved.

Everything became silent and still.

All eyes were on the small boy's body clad in a red cassock[9] and white surplice[10] of the typical server of those times. He lay there in a crumpled heap, his blond hair, usually bobbing in the breeze as he hurried along, now still; his right hand pointing to the altar; his left under him; his hazel eyes closed; his breathing, usually rapid, now shallow; his face white as chalk.

Father Rahshock, stunned for a moment, knelt down at Ciesiu's side, felt the boy's pulse, then picked him up gently and drew him close to his heart and carried him into the sacristy.[11] Father Franek, the young assistant pastor, was there getting ready to hear confessions, since it was past 6 o'clock. He hurried out, retrieved the fallen sprinkler, and blest the baskets, showering them with holy water. By now Ciesiu had been tenderly placed on the priest's own bench; Sister Sylvestra was rubbing Ciesiu's hands briskly. She laid a cold, wet towel on the feverish brow of the unconscious boy. It was then that the priest noticed how thin Ciesiu was—and how thin and worn were his clothes. The shoes showed holes in the soles.

9. Cass-ock: garment similar to the priest's robe.
10. Sir-plus: a cotton, sometimes lace shirt, worn over the cassock.
11. Sac-ris-tee: part of the church where the sacred vessels, vestments, etc., are kept.

Slowly Ciesiu began to stir, to sigh, to flutter his eyelids, to come to. He was given a cup of hot chocolate, known then as "cocoa," to drink. When assured Ciesiu was all right, Father walked him home across the school playground, his hand on the youngster's shoulder.

At the curb waited a well-dressed man holding a huge Easter basket. Ciesiu vividly remembers the man's hat. It was a derby, very popular in the thirties, usually black or brown. This derby, however, was purple.[12] The man spoke up, serious and seemingly concerned, "Father, please take my basket and leave it with this boy's family. They can use it more than I can." He patted his large, round tummy, which hid an even larger heart. Then he tipped his hat to the priest, put his arm around Ciesiu's neck, squeezed it with his big, broad hand, and walked away. He disappeared around the corner. Neither priest nor server had ever seen him before. They wondered if they would meet again.

That night there was also a box of chocolates for Ciesiu's family from Sister Sylvestra. Sister Superior remarked to Sister Sylvestra, "Usually we share gifts with the other Sisters in our community. This year we will share this sweet gift with Ciesiu's folks."

Meanwhile the Reverend Rahshock picked up the phone in his rectory[13] and talked to his friend, Mr.

---

12. Purple is a Lenten color in the Church's liturgy (see footnote 12a) but a popular color outside the Church during the Easter season and all of spring.

12a. Lit-er-gee: the Church's various services and ceremonies, especially the Holy Sacrifice of the Mass.

13. Rek-tor-ree: the priest's home.

Casey Kania of the Archy Avenue Clothing Store. He outlined a number of details to him. By 8 p.m. Mr. Kania was at Ciesiu's home, delivering new clothes for all there. He grinned broadly as Ciesiu's *tatus*[14] tried to protest, declaring they couldn't accept charity because "there are people poorer than we are. They should have these clothes." Mr. Kania shook his head, then shook dad's hand and pushed the parcels with the clothing into the arms of Ciesiu's mother, who had just come to the door. "God works in His own marvelous and mysterious ways. He wishes you to have this clothing. A friend of His has already paid for it." With those words he left.

Father Rahshock and Sister Sylvestra applauded Ciesiu and his family when they appeared the next morning for the Easter Sunrise Mass. Ciesiu, his parents, brother, and two sisters looked so neat in their new Easter outfits.

Somewhere a man sat down to a breakfast of bacon and eggs. He was well dressed. On a hook hung his hat, a purple derby. He cocked his head at his plate and reflected how luscious that blest Polish ham, sausage, and bread must taste at Ciesiu's house.

He smiled a big satisfied smile.

"*Smacznego!*"[15] He toasted Ciesiu, raising a steaming cup of coffee.

Perhaps elsewhere, somewhere above, the heavenly choirs were answering him and Ciesiu,

"*Wesolego!*[16] Alleluja! Happy Easter!"

14. Tah-toosh: Polish for "daddy."
15. Smah-chneh-go: Polish for "May it taste good!"
16. Veh-sow-wag-go: Polish for "joyful."

The Little Flower

Phyllis was to receive her First Holy Communion[1] on Palm Sunday, as was customary for the children of Five Polish Martyrs Parish. This way the communicants could walk in procession four times—before Mass when entering the church, during Mass when receiving the Blest Palm and again when receiving Holy Communion, and, finally, after Mass when leaving church to have their pictures taken and be congratulated by their family and friends.

1. Come-union: receiving Jesus under the form of bread and wine. Jesus gave His Apostles their First Communion this way on Holy Thursday Night.

Phyllis felt very proud and pleased that she was able to receive Jesus for the first time! How she longed to have Him come to her as He did when her parents, older brothers, and sisters went to the altar on Sundays while she had to stay in her pew.[2] She was the youngest at home, so she was last to be taught about receiving Communion and to be trained to live as a good Christian (that is, as a loving and loyal follower of Christ).[3]

However, in her great excitement over her First Holy Communion on Palm Sunday, Phyllis failed to think more deeply about her First Confession,[4] which was to take place the Saturday before her Big Day. She felt so happy, so hungry for Holy Communion that somehow First Confession didn't seem so important, especially since she didn't judge she had hurt Jesus by any really serious sins.

So Phyllis went to confession, now called Reconciliation[5] because we are reconciled with God (that is, made friends again with Him by being sorry for our sins of disobedience, lack of love, etc.). Phyllis confessed her little sins as best as she could remember them. The priest was so nice and friendly to all who came to confession. For Phyllis, however, it was First Holy Communion that mattered most.

But when she received her God, Jesus, the next day, she suddenly felt sorry she didn't make a better confession. She realized as Jesus came to her that she could have told two certain sins that weren't so little—not big, but again not so little either. Gone was the joy of being

---

2. Pue: bench in church to sit on.
3. Cry-st: another name for Jesus.
4. Con-fess-shun: telling your sins to the priest, who takes God's place.
5. Reck-con-sill-lee-aye-shun: same as confession, above.

united with her God. Gone was the "high" of having received the most important sacrament[6] after Baptism[7] because she didn't receive the sacrament of Reconciliation more properly, more thoughtfully, with greater preparation.

Phyllis promised Jesus there and then that she would make a second confession, a really good one next Saturday, the day before Easter. This time she prepared more prayerfully and more humbly.[8] She then confessed of not being totally honest and open to God because she didn't look at herself (that is, into her heart) as sincerely as she ought.

Again, the priest was kind and consoling (that is, comforting). He explained her two sins were not so serious after all, but it would have been better had she mentioned them the first time. He then gave her absolution[9] and a small penance[10]: two Our Fathers, two Hail Marys, and two good deeds to be done in Easter week to some person, young or old.

When Phyllis found her favorite pew again she felt she should also talk to Jesus' Mother as she had already talked so much with Her Son. She asked Mary to forgive her too since it was Mary's Son, Jesus, who died for our sins.

Easter Sunday dawned rosy and resplendent[11] with fresh dew on fragrant flowers, especially the violets,

---

6. Sack-rah-ment: a sacred thing; one of seven such in the Catholic Church.
7. Bap-tis-sym: the Sacrament by which one becomes a Christian.
8. Hum-blee: not proud or uppity.
9. Ab-sol-lu-shun: forgiveness.
10. Pen-nance: making up for one's sins.
11. Ree-splen-dent: glorious, glittering.

daffodils, crocuses, which were all in their spring finery. In church, lilies were everywhere, in pots covered with gold and silver tinfoil, in gaily colored baskets, in stone and metal vases. Phyllis' family attended the early Mass, known sometimes as the Sunrise Service. The priest spoke in his homily[12] about Jesus returning to life, how Nature comes back to life, how we should return to share in God's life if we lost that life by sinning.

Soon it was time for Phyllis to receive her second Holy Communion. This time she felt not so much a thrill as last Sunday but rather a deep sense of peace and gratitude.[13] "How great God is; how small I am. Yet He loves me so much," Phyllis said in her heart. Now the priest stood before her. Poised in his holy hand was the Host[14]—a tiny thin wafer of bread, yet God Himself!

As Phyllis lifted her own little hands to receive the Sacred Host and as the priest bent to place Jesus reverently on those girlish outstretched palms, he lost his balance slightly. The Host fluttered to the floor. As it did, it touched the skirt of the young miss. Instead of panicking,[15] Phyllis felt a wonderful, strange, ecstatic[16] joy. Seeing Jesus lying there on the church floor, Phyllis quickly received It into her. The priest nodded his approval[17] and said as usual, "The Body of Christ," to which Phyllis fervently replied, "Amen," meaning "I believe. It is so."

12. Hom-mil-lee: sermon, talk by the priest in church.
13. Grat-tit-tude: thankfulness.
14. Hoe-st: round wafer of thin bread that becomes Jesus on the altar during Mass or the Liturgy, as it's also called.
15. Pan-nick-ing: getting very scared and excited.
16. Ek-stat-tic: deep, deep happiness.
17. Ap-prove-all: acknowledging something as all right or okay.

As last Sunday, so now the comely[18] communicant was again in ecstasy. How she told Jesus she loved Him as she knelt[19] in her pew, eyes closed, her heart aflame. There and then she made another promise—to do some kind deed for love of Jesus to some poor person and for Mary, the Mother of Jesus. Phyllis vowed[20] she would make a shrine[21] in Her honor. Many people have shrines in their backyards or on the front lawn, even in their homes. What an excellent idea! She would think of Jesus as often as she came by the shrine and thank His Mother for giving Him to us on Christmas Day.

Now Phyllis had a pretty good idea how she would make her shrine. It was late April so she knew she could dig some small rocks out of the soft soil in her backyard. Mother and dad said she could have the southwest corner, so she began digging there. Her father helped her nail together three boards, two-and-a-half feet long and six inches wide, so that they resembled a wooden triangle. A piece of plywood was fitted into the back. Then he mixed cement for the floor of the shrine. Phyllis trowelled[22] the leftover cement on the inner sides of the three boards. Then the newly dug stones were set in the wet cement to resemble a grotto.[23]

18. Com-lee: pretty, cute.
19. Nelt: was on one's knees.
20. Vowd: made a solemn, serious promise.
21. Sh-rine: a sacred nook or space for a statue of a holy person.
22. Trow-weld: spread out with a trowel, which is a small, flat, hand tool.
23. Grot-toe: Man's first shrines were usually in rocky caves or in open, hollowed-out mountains and hills where stones stick out of the walls.

How proud and pleased were Phyllis' parents as they perceived[24] their daughter's dogged[25] determination[26] and her dream come true! Phyllis felt elated and thanked God for the happy inspiration[27] to construct[28] the shrine. She said, wondering aloud, "Wouldn't flowers look lovely if planted here in front of the shrine?" Dad and mom looked at each other with a knowing smile. They had the same thought. They nodded to each other. Mother hurried to the house and came out with dad's Easter present to her—a Sweetheart rosebush! The roses had already bloomed but would bloom again if given plenty of sunlight and water. Dad immediately pulled the rosebush out of the flowerpot and planted it in front of the shrine just where Phyllis indicated. It swayed there in the morning breeze as if surprised, yet enjoying the bright outdoors.

Even though the shrine was finished, it lacked the most important item of all—the statue of Jesus' Mother. This time her parents stated firmly, "Phyllis, you're on your own now. We helped you enough. You'll have to earn your own money to buy the figure of Mary. You will appreciate this shrine even more if you do odd jobs, run errands for people, babysit and save some of your allowance. Each time you pray before the shrine later on, you'll know the statue in it was obtained by your own hard work."

24. Per-sieved: saw.
25. Dog-ged: not wanting to give up (like a dog holding on to something or someone by the teeth and not letting go).
26. Dee-ter-min-nay-shun: strong desire to reach a certain goal.
27. In-spir-ra-shun: beautiful idea.
28. Kon-struct: build, make.

Phyllis thought this a neat idea although she was disappointed the shrine would be without a statue for some time. It would take weeks, perhaps months, to earn enough even for a statue only two feet high. Statues were expensive, especially in Phyllis' day. But she was a girl of faith, faithful to her promise. So she babysat, mowed lawns for neighbors and friends, read to elderly folk whose eyesight was failing and fading. She performed services even when people couldn't give her much—sometimes nothing at all when the poor couldn't pay her.

In the meantime the Sweetheart roses budded, bloomed, and lost their petals—only to begin the process all over again as roses usually do. However, the center rose of the plant for some mysterious reason never faded, never wilted, never died. It remained fresh, fragrant, and as full as if it had just burst into being. Phyllis marvelled but said nothing except to praise God.

Three months passed.

Finally Phyllis had enough money saved to buy that longed-for figure of Mary. Swiftly she skipped down the street, whistling like a lark. Her pigtails were streaming behind her like two TV antennae bent backward. Her fair, freckled face was flushed with excitement, her faintly brown eyes flashing in delight, her hand clutching the five crumpled dollar bills that represented her three-month's earnings.

She fairly flew to the religious goods store, which was named as such because you could buy Bibles, statues, candles, and all kinds of things needed for a shrine, church, chapel,[29] or school. The kindly but curious old owner of the store peered over his horn-rimmed glasses

---

29. Chap-pal: small church as in a monastery, convent, or school.

and pointed to the shelves toward the rear as Phyllis breathlessly inquired where he kept statues. There must have been a hundred of them—but there on the very center shelf stood a novel[30] statue, the likes of which Phyllis had never seen in her life. "My, such a sweet face on this statue. I just love that brown veil[31] and cloak Mary is wearing." She turned to the shopkeeper. "I want that one!" she shouted, pointing to the admired statue. "It's really neat!"

Carefully, as if carrying eggs, Phyllis carried the twenty-five-inch box containing the statue heavily wrapped in tissue paper directly to the shrine.

The lone rose that never drooped or died was standing smartly in the center of the bush as Phyllis arrived. Faded petals of other roses lay strewn[32] on the ground.

When she had positioned the statue in the empty shrine, Phyllis knelt down to pray to Jesus and His Blessed Mother Mary. Then she dashed into the house exclaiming, "Mom! Mom! Come see the statue I bought!"

Mother hurried out of her room and outside, looked at the statue, looked again, shook her head in disbelief,[33] turned to stare at her daughter, then broke the silence to say very slowly, "Phyllis, I'm sorry to tell you this—but that's not a statue of Mary."

"It isn't?" cried the young miss, mystified, startled. "Then who is it?"

---

30. Nov-ell: unusual, new kind.
31. Vayle: head covering instead of a hat or cap, worn especially by nuns, brides, women, and girls.
32. Strew-n: scattered.
33. Dis-bee-leaf: unwilling to believe.

"It's a statue of St. Theresa," replied mother in a muffled, strained voice.

"Who, who is St. Theresa?" asked Phyllis, her lips quivering[34] and her eyes filling with tears.

Mother replied, "St. Theresa was a young saint, a nun[35] who promised she would send a shower of roses, or blessings, upon earth after she was dead."

"A shower of roses," echoed Phyllis. Then she practically shrieked with delight.[36]

"Oh, Mother, now I know why that middle rose has bloomed for three months!"

"Bloomed for three months?" It was mother's turn to echo a reply. "I didn't know God had performed a little miracle[37] here. You didn't know—of course, how could you know?—but St. Theresa has another name. She is called The Little Flower!"

Phyllis never returned the statue.

She kept it in her shrine.

Now when she prays, she prays to Jesus, Mary, and The Little Flower.

---

34. Quiv-er-ing: trembling.
35. Religious woman living in a convent or monastery and serving God as a teacher, nurse, etc.
36. Dee-light: great joy.
37. Meer-a-call: a marvelous deed that God alone can do by Himself or through others.

The Uniform

Chester wanted a boy scout uniform so badly! He had become a scout several months ago but was too poor to afford five dollars, the cost of a complete scouting outfit in the depression days. He felt out of place with his fellow second-class scouts because he was wearing ordinary, everyday clothes at the weekly patrol meetings. Worse, a campout was scheduled after Easter and only uniformed boys would be permitted to attend.

Chester was desperate. He had never been to Camp McDonard, outside of Chicago, where he lived. How he wanted to see the countryside, stay by the lake, and see spring flowers and budding trees in the forest where the scouts would be encamped! At twelve years of age Chester had seen nothing but the usual city sites: asphalt and concrete, houses huddled next to each other, dust and dirt, and the rumbling traffic of streetcars, trucks, and autos.

Time and again Chester asked his parents, "Please buy me a scout's uniform." Each time Dad sadly shook his head while his mother wiped tears from her eyes—and Chester's. The answer was always a sorrowful, "Son, we just don't have the money for anything but food, the mortgage on the house, and the ordinary clothes we need to wear. You would look wonderful in a uniform, but it can't be done. Someday, when times get better, we will get you one, but not now."

Chester's patrol leader, Johnnie Cut, was also anxious to see all his scouts in uniform. He talked to the troop leader, Joe Buck, but no one had volunteered to sponsor even one scout. Money was scarce; many people were out of work while those with jobs were poorly paid. Because of this, Chester couldn't even find anyone who would employ him to clean up their yards, cut their grass, or run their errands. True, the boy had a paper route, but the three dollars a week he earned helped buy food for the family; that's how hard times were then. Children often contributed to the upkeep of the home in their own little ways, such as peddling daily newspapers or selling them on street corners.

THE UNIFORM

On Holy Saturday evening, April 19, while helping his two sisters and brother color Easter eggs, Chester heard his scouting friends calling him in front of the house. In ethnic neighborhoods, especially in those days, young people hardly ever visited each other in their homes. They simply called for you by loudly shouting your name outside your house. This was perhaps because families were large (eight to ten children) and homes were rather crowded. The kitchen table was the place where the family ate meals, the children did their homework, and dad read his evening paper. Bedrooms were small and narrow with no desk and shared among brothers and sisters.

Chester peeked out of the window from behind the curtains, saw his buddies in their uniforms—some new—and immediately walked back to the table. He could hardly refrain from crying. His brother and sisters guessed what this meant. They knew how much the uniform meant to him.

His friends kept calling and calling. Chester's siblings[1] kept glancing at him, hinting he should answer in some way. Chester just couldn't find the courage to do so; he was so heartbroken. Finally, his friends left, regretting that their friend had not answered.

Next morning, Easter Sunday, unfortunately turned out gray, gloomy, and foggy. The drab color matched Chester's mood when he should have been rejoicing at Christ's Resurrection and celebrating the suffering, crucified Saviour's return to life.

---

1. Sib-leengs: sisters and brothers.

He served the 5 a.m. Mass, often called the
Sunrise Service, tried to enjoy the Allelujas[2], the lilies,
and the colorful Easter bonnets many women wore.
All the altar boys received chocolate bunnies and
marshmallow eggs. That helped.

Then came the sweet surprise!

Waiting for Chester by the crowded church
doors were his troop leader, Joe Buck, his patrol
leader, Johnnie Cut, and all his friends in full scout
uniforms, full of smiles and friendly laughter. This *was*
a surprise—and an embarrassment—for Chester. He
didn't expect his friends to meet him with smiles after
he failed to respond to their calls last night.

But there they were.

At a nod from his troop leader, Johnnie Cut
brought forward a cardboard box from behind his
back. "Here, Chester, is your uniform! Last night
every boy who couldn't afford a uniform received one.
The local merchants on Archey Avenue paid for
them. That's why your friends went to your house last
night!"

Delighted at the gift but dismayed at his behavior
the night before, Chester blushed to the roots of his
unruly blond hair.

"Thank you, thank you all," he said shyly. Then
turning in the direction of the church and the
Resurrected Redeemer within, he added in his very
devout, usual manner, "Thank you, Jesus, for
Easter—and for kind friends!"

"Cree, cree!" The call of the Flying Eagle Patrol,
Chester's patrol, was his friends' reply. One dear little

2.   Ahl-lay-loo-yah: "Praise the Lord!"

old lady, standing close by, turned in surprise and remarked, "This must be a new Easter custom! I prefer Alleluja instead!" Everybody laughed.

Troops 006 and 007 moved out of the parish playing ground on Easter Monday in rather ragged marching formation. The scouts were not yet fully trained, but all the boys were in uniform with knapsacks on their backs, overstuffed with their blankets, towels, toothbrushes, and whatever else they were able to push into them. They boarded three buses and drove southward to Camp McDonard. Many, as Chester, had never been further than the city limits.

In contrast to yesterday's wet weather, the day was bright, beautiful, the sun drying everything it touched with its golden rays. The buses rolled through flat but fertile fields and small towns quaint and quiet with their general stores and one-story homes; then to the forest preserves where they would camp for a week.

Such hustle and bustle, meeting other troops, getting cabins assigned and schedules reviewed! Finally, before supper, around 7 p.m., everyone was free to look around. It was too late and too cold to go swimming in Lake McDonard, so most scouts went into the woods, fresh with violets, daffodils, and crocuses[3] covering the forest floor.

Chester was irresistibly[4] and mysteriously drawn to the lake. He found a small, blossoming apple tree with a convenient, low fork in the branches for him to

3. Crow-cuss-sess: flowers, golden-yellow in color
4. Ir-riss-siss-tab-lee: beyond the power to say "no."

climb into and sit. The sun was sinking slowly in the west, and the lake shimmered in its setting shafts of intense, glowing colors of crimson, orange, and gold. All was so quiet, so peaceful. Voices of scouts faded in the forest. Chester found himself all alone.

But not quite.

Not in the usual sense of "all alone."

Chester, in this sylvan[5] setting of a background and the lake in the foreground, amid Nature's great, glorious outdoors, thought of God, Author and Creator of Nature. He felt as he once felt when he was in the second grade. His Aunt Rose had come by to visit his family. Aunt Rose was Chester's mom's younger sister. She asked Chester what he would like to be. Before he could say, "A priest of God," his aunt whispered, slowly, simply, as if she read his heart, "You will be a priest." Later Chester learnt that this statement was a sort of prophecy. He felt so thrilled, so excited that someone else knew his secret. Chester was afraid to reveal his secret to anyone, thinking they might laugh or think he was trying to be "uppity" or better than they.

Now he felt that same feeling of elation[6] and exaltation.[7] God, he felt, wanted him indeed to be His priest. He agreed. He would try to become a good priest like the priests in his parish, Father Alfie, Father Stanley, and others before them.

5. Sill-van: refers to a forest, woods.
6. Ee-lay-shun: lifted up in spirit, delighted.
7. Eggs-salt-tay-shun: much happiness.

"Cree! Cree!" Chester heard his patrol leader summon his scouts. "Cree! Cree!" the call of the Flying Eagle Patrol was heard from the forest.

Chester stirred in the fork of the tree where he had received his precious call, his vocation. He slid down the trunk, plucked a few apple blossoms, examined them with admiration, smiled, made a trumpet out of his right hand, and cried out in return, "Cree! Cree! Cree!"

Under his breath he added joyfully, "Alleluja! Praise the Lord!"

The Swing

Carol was babysitting her cousin Kim. It was an unusually mild day for March, so Carol permitted Kim to enjoy the outdoors on grandma's back porch. Kim's grandmother was also Carol's aunt.

Kim loved to swing on grandma's porch. Carol dutifully helped her little charge by gently and carefully pushing the swing back and forth, much to the delight of the youngster tightly hanging on the ropes. Carol was conscientious[1] about her babysitting

---

1. Con-she-en-shus: doing good because your conscience (con-shunce) tells you to do so.

duties. She was asked to babysit often as she was such a responsible person, though only ten years old. She was also an attractive girl of medium height, beautiful brown eyes, auburn hair, and slim build.

Now, Kim was five years old, a chubby child with dark hair and eyes, hyperactive[2], self-willed, and disobedient. She frequently did little mischievous[3] things just to test her elders and babysitters—or simply because she was bored and wanted to "do her own thing."

So, she suddenly decided in mid-swing to let go of the ropes and see if she could land with both feet on the floor without falling. "Whee!" she shrilled as she sailed off the swing and crashed, crumpled to the floor, hurt. Then she began to scream both in agony at the pain and in anger that she failed to accomplish her unworthy purpose.

Out of the kitchen flew grandma, alarmed and anxious to know what happened! Through her tearful, bleary, moist baby eyes, Kim saw her grandparent rushing to her aid. Kim screamed louder, not in pain but to gain attention and sympathy. Carol, in the meantime, just stood there, stunned at this unexpected turn of events. She became even more surprised and startled when Kim pointed an accusing finger at Carol shouting, "She did it! Carol pushed me off the swing. Carol is mean! I hate her! I hate her!"

Dumbfounded at this second unusual event (being wrongfully accused), Carol continued to stand as if a statue carved out of stone. Kim's false

2. Hi-per: overly active, too active, constantly "on the go."
3. Miss-chuf-vus: naughty, getting into mischief (miss-chuf).

accusation caused Carol's cheeks to burn as if she really were guilty. Grandma, seeing that Kim was bleeding from her fall, began to soothe the child, clucking over her like a mother hen over a frightened or injured chick. Her lean, long body bent easily as in one continuous motion she stooped and gathered Kim into her arms and carried the little girl into the kitchen. Then she began to wash away the dirt from Kim's bruised knees and elbows. Noticing that the injuries were not so severe, grandma turned on Carol, scolding and criticizing her for being mean and lacking manners, believing the big lie that Kim told her.

A third blow for Carol! Even her aunt had turned against her! She finally found her tongue and began to protest her innocence while handing grandma Band-Aids for Kim's bruises. She explained how Kim had deliberately let go of the ropes and had even shouted "Whee!" as she jumped off the swing. Her exasperated[4] and angry aunt was in no mood to listen to what she thought was a lame excuse on the part of her niece, Carol. And Kim kept blaming Carol so as to escape blame for what was really Kim's fault.

Grandma grimly finished ministering to her granddaughter. Then, silently and solemnly, she marched into the living room, indicating to both girls to follow. She approached the bookcase, reached to the top shelf, and took down the largest tome[5] there. It was the Bible. Without a word she placed the Holy Book on the table, turned to Carol and demanded, "If

4. Eggs-zas-pore-rated: out of sorts or out of temper, vexed.
5. Toe-m: another word for "book," usually meaning a large one.

you're so innocent, swear on this Bible that you didn't push Kim off the swing. Then, and only then, will I believe you."

Carol almost jumped at the opportunity to prove her innocence this way. She reverenced and regarded the Bible as God's Word, His Message and the Good News. But because she also realized how serious it is to swear to the truth on the Bible, she suddenly became afraid and confused. "Supposing I was responsible in some way for Kim's fall? Maybe I pushed too hard. I can't swear that it wasn't my fault if I did something that wasn't exactly right. I just don't know what to do now."

Carol again stood there rigid as a pole. Finally, she shook her head again in confusion and ran up the stairs, tears streaming from her eyes. It was bad enough to be accused falsely by her cousin, but worse not to be believed by her aunt.

"You pack your bag right now!" yelled grandma after her. "I'm sending you home this very minute. Your mother will hear of your bad behavior as soon as I phone her!"

In her grief Carol remembered it was Good Friday. She recalled how someone else once was wrongly accused on the first Good Friday. That Someone was Jesus. And like Jesus, Carol too suffered, not crucifixion[6] but being painfully whipped by her mother on arriving home. Her mom also sent Carol to bed without supper. Never had Carol been so misjudged, mistreated, and miserable. Only the

6. Crew-suh-fix-shun: being nailed to a cross.

thought of Jesus being whipped, crucified, and hung hungry on the Cross helped her control her sobs of sorrow and sadness.

Next day was Holy Saturday. By now everybody in the house and in the neighborhood had heard about Carol taking a beating and being grounded by her mother. "How odd!" Carol reflected,[7] "Everybody thought Jesus was guilty too—except His family and friends. But even my own family and friends consider me guilty. I'll suffer this for Jesus' sake." That night she fell into a troubled sleep once more, tears staining her pillow. "At least I have a soft bed," she whispered to Jesus, "and a warm blanket. You had only a hard, wooden cross and a crown of thorns upon your head—and no warm covering at all."

Easter Sunday dawned bright and beautiful even though the branches on the trees were still bare. It was March 31. Carol and her family went to church, but she just couldn't rejoice at the glad Allelujas[8] or at the sight of the golden gleam of candles on the altar or oh, the array of lilies sprouting in the awesome sanctuary.[9] She was still experiencing the pains of her "Good Friday," but she managed to smile as she realized Jesus was alive and risen, no longer suffering His Good Friday.

That afternoon Carol became alive again (that is, in spirit) and was able to rejoice with the Risen Christ after all.

---

7. Ree-flec-ted: thought over what happened.
8. Ah-lay-loo-yahs: "Praise the Lord."
9. Sank-chew-airy: the front of the church where services take place. Also sometimes the church itself.

Why?

What happened?

Well, like all naughty children, Kim tried her tricks once too often. On Easter Sunday afternoon, Kim tried to fool even Carol's own mother, who was now Kim's new babysitter. As Carol's mother was pushing the swing in which Kim sat, yes, you guessed it, Kim let go of the ropes, shouted "Whee!" and jumped squealing to the floor, falling again.

This time there was no Carol to blame.

Kim had learnt a painful lesson. She would never let go of the ropes and blame someone else again.

Carol forgave her as did her aunt and mother, as a good Christian should.

Easter Sunday, therefore, became again what it was intended to be: a coming back to life, to a life of forgiving and loving, even though wrongly accused by those you love.

Mother's Day

Chester was again at the boy scout camp. It was a
year after his first experience camping out. He loved
the great and glorious outdoors: the clear, quiet air; the
shimmering lake where he had encountered[1] God in
that special way; and the woods fragrant with flowers
and filled with blossoms of every sort. It was the second
week of May and the forest floor was one massive
carpet of purple. Violets everywhere! Never had
Chester seen so many of these tiny, pretty plants in all
his life! He picked his way carefully over the bare spots
so as not to crush these delicate, floral[2] creatures. He

1. En-cown-terd: met.
2. Floor-roll: flowery.

plucked one or two of the violets, which valiantly clung close to the still damp earth, to examine their beauty with awe[3] and wonder. "How good God is to give us such lovely, remarkable beauty in such an out-of-the-way place! Hardly anyone sees these fine flowers except the scouts who come here," he said to himself.

Then another thought struck him. Sunday was Mother's Day. He would be back home tomorrow, Saturday evening, in time for supper. Why not bring mom some of these forest beauties?

But how?

He pondered[4] and puzzled over the problem of taking home a big bunch of violets before they wilted and died. He said a little prayer for guidance, but nothing happened.

That afternoon, however, as his patrol was hiking along the edge of the lake, the answer came. The different troops and patrols were being drilled in proper marching procedures[5] on this particular weekend at Camp McDonard. Chester missed a step in his excitement but managed to catch up and march in formation again.

Chester galvanized[6] into action as soon as the scouts returned for their cookout in the woods.

He went first to the camp commander to ask permission to talk to the cook. The commander was a kind, quiet man with children of his own. Since he was

---

3. Aw: great respect.
4. Pond-derd: thought deeply about.
5. Pro-see-jurs: ways and methods of doing things correctly.
6. Gal-van-ized: became excitedly active.

such a good father at home, he knew how to relate[7] to the scouts. Chester said he wanted to surprise his mother with a "homemade gift" but he needed a few simple items[8] from the kitchen. The commander gazed at the blond, brown-eyed, sturdy, short scout and nodded in agreement, pleasantly impressed.[9]

Cook was surprised at Chester's request. "You want what?" he asked twice as the bashful boy explained his needs. "Okay, I think I can help you." Ordinarily, scouts came to the camp kitchen only to help with dishes and to serve meals—or to ask for snacks when these ran out during free time.

So wiping his hands on his apron, cook went to the pantry,[10] found several medium-size baskets used on tables for bread and rolls. Chester selected one, a pretty white and blue basket about twenty inches round. Next, cook got for him an old, ragged but clean dish towel and a small roll of wax paper (plastic wrap had not been invented yet). He rummaged[11] through a table drawer and brought out a handful of rubber bands. He gave these to the boy, smiling at this eager beaver of a scout who had come to his kitchen with such an unusual request.

Saturday afternoon was free time because camp was breaking up at 4 p.m. Chester had packed his knapsack[12] and with other scouts tidied up the cabins

7. Ree-late: get along with and understand.
8. Eye-tems: things.
9. Im-pressed: clearly touched by something or someone.
10. Pan-tree: storage place for food supplies and table needs.
11. Rum-maged: sorted through with one's hand.
12. Nap-sack: a pack carried on one's back.

and cleaned up the grounds. Campfires were carefully doused with water and the ashes covered with dirt to prevent forest fires.

Now Chester was able to carry out the plan God had inspired in him earlier that morning. He took the white and blue basket, the dishtowel, the roll of wax paper, and the rubber bands and hurried out to the woods. Cautiously he tiptoed through the fields of violets, gently plucked the largest but those not yet in full bloom, and placed them gingerly[13] in the basket till it was full. Then, just as carefully, he made his way to the nearby brook. It was gurgling and racing, cool, clear, sparkling with an early spring spirit. Chester sat down on a grassy knoll.[14] Slowly he emptied his basket on the banks of the stream. He then tore the dishcloth and wax paper into three-inch strips. The cloth was dipped into the stream, then wrapped around a bunch of violets and covered over with the waxed paper. Thus, each bunch of violets became a small, well-preserved package of fresh flowers secured by the rubber bands and lovingly laid in the basket in circles. The lad had made a bouquet of woodland violets.

Chester barely had time now to put the precious basket in a cardboard box he found outside the camp commander's cabin. Other scouts had boxes filled with souvenirs or botanical[15] and insect specimens[16] that they had gathered when exploring the forest.

Chester returned home at 6:15 p.m.

13. Gin-jer-lee: carefully.
14. Nole: a little heap or mound.
15. Bo-tan-nickel: having to do with plants, flowers, etc.
16. Spes-sim-mens: examples, samples.

What a surprise he had for mother!

Such a smile on her face as her son opened the box and showed her the basket full of fragrant, fresh, forest flowers!

Tears glistened in her eyes, ran down her worn cheeks, and splashed like rain on the violets, as if watering and refreshing them.

Chester's hands trembled as his mother took the precious present that her son had so thoughtfully prepared for her.

"She likes it!" he shouted to himself.

Mother kissed Chester on both cheeks.

"What a wonderful Mother's Day gift," she repeated happily. "I never received such a lovely present in my whole life, if I remember rightly, except once when your father brought me roses. But he bought those. You picked these with your own hands and made a beautiful bouquet of them all by yourself! There ought to be a merit badge in floral arrangements. You would get it for sure!"

Years passed.

Chester was now a young man of twenty-two. He found himself in the woods again on a May morning. He was no longer a scout. He was now a seminarian,[17] attending a seminary[18] forty miles from his home in Chicago. It was surrounded by woods with a lake at its center, just like good old Camp McDonard.

Memories flooded Chester's mind of those happy scouting days. He recalled the violets he picked for his

17. Sem-min-nare-ree-an: a student of the priesthood, living and attending a special school for future priests.
18. Sem-min-nary: a school that prepares students for the priesthood.

51

dear mom as he looked at another purple carpet of violets before him here in the seminary forest.

A new thought struck him.

He was shrine master that semester.[19] This meant that he was assigned to look after the shrine[20] on the second floor of the building where the seminarians studied, slept, and lived. It was his duty to keep candles lit before the shrine in the evening during the great holidays of Christmas, Easter, etc. He also placed flowers before the shrine: cut flowers delivered in winter; fresh flowers gathered by the shrine master in spring and autumn in the woods where Chester now stood. The shrine consisted of a beautiful painting of the Madonna (that is, Mary the Mother of God) by a famous Italian artist. She was pictured on this particular canvas with the boy Jesus on her right and the boy John the Baptizer (Jesus' cousin) on her left.

Shrine masters were expected to trim their flowers and arrange them artistically[21] in glass or metal vases. Cleaned and trimmed candles were then placed on either side of the Marian painting.

Chester thought of the Mother's Day basket he had put together at Camp McDonard and presented to his mom on returning home from camp. "I couldn't do this now," he said sadly to himself.

But he could do something similar.[22]

An idea had flashed into his mind, like an electric bulb lighting up at the flick of the switch.

---

19. Sem-mess-ter: one half of the school year.
20. Sh-ryne: a sacred place of prayer other than a church or chapel.
21. Art-tiss-tick-lee: with good taste and in a pleasing pattern.
22. Sym-mill-lair: something nearly the same.

He galvanized into action—as he did once when a boy scout.

He hurried to the prefect, the priest in charge of the boys and the building, and asked permission to go not to the kitchen, as at Camp McDonard, but to the chemistry[23] laboratory.[24] He explained to Father Prefect it had something to do with the shrine. Permission was granted by the tall, dark-haired, middle-aged priest.

In the laboratory, or lab for short, Chester took as many small glass jars as he could find. He neatly lined them up in rows of ten in a wooden apple box and went back to the woods. He sat down by a small stream and dipped the two-inch jars in the still, silent water. Then he slowly plucked handfuls of violets that grew around the creek and placed them into the cute containers. When he had filled all of them, he replaced them in the box and turned toward the building and its shrine.

That night, as the Seminarians came up from the chapel on the first floor, the first thing that greeted their eyes as they reached the second floor landing was a low altar[25] covered with a white linen cloth standing in front of the shrine.

On the altar spelled out with violets in their little water jars were six large letters forming the loving word, MOTHER.

---

23. Kem-miss-tree: the science and study of chemicals.
24. Lab-bore-rat-tore-ree: where chemicals are kept and studied.
25. All-ter: a table-like stand in church for sacred services.

The boys paused, stopped to gaze in wonder at the floral display, dropped to their knees, and prayed for their mothers.

They now realized tomorrow was Mother's Day.

Chester was the last student to come up. He, too, knelt to pray for his mom. He felt a hand on his shoulder. It was Father Fred, the prefect. Tears were gleaming in his large, dark eyes.

He smiled through his tears and in a low, reverent[26] tone remarked, "Thank you, Chester, for remembering our mothers in this special way."

That was the happiest Mother's Day remembrance Chester ever had—except, of course, the one when he returned from Camp McDonard with violets for his own dear mom.

---

26. Rev-veh-rent: full of respect.

White Shoes

Ciesiu[1] was preparing for his First Holy
Communion.[2] As a matter of fact, he was in the same
class as Phyllis,[3] whom we met in a previous story. Like
her, Ciesiu couldn't wait to receive Jesus on First
Communion Day. As yet he didn't know he wanted to be
a priest some day, but he sure loved to listen to his teacher
as she told the children how good God is, how He created
the world and sent His Son Jesus to us, how Jesus lived
on this earth first with His Holy Family and then with His
followers, who were called Apostles[4].

1. Chesh-shoo: Polish for Chester.
2. Come-union.
3. Fill-iss: the little girl in the story "The Little Flower," found elsewhere in this
   book.
4. Up-paw-soles.

Sister Maxima[5] was the First Communion teacher. "Maxima" means "big"—and Sister was *big!* She seemed as wide as she was tall—well, almost. To the children, Sister seemed to fill the classroom with her large presence and to tower over everything, like Mount Hood in Portland, Oregon, where later Ciesiu was a priest. Big as Sister Maxima was in body, she was bigger in heart and soul. She was always smiling no matter how naughty or noisy the children became, even on restless, tiring afternoons. Her round face was ever crinkled[6] in a smile and her large, limpid[7] gray eyes always sparkled with joy and love for the children, their parents, their school. She was the soul of patience, piety[8], practical[9] wisdom, peaceful bearing. She walked quietly and gracefully despite her huge build and cumbersome[10] nun's clothing. You would be awed at the sight of her—but never afraid.

Now the word "Maxima" also means "the greatest." Sister Maxima was indeed the greatest teacher to her pupils,[11] the greatest stand-in mother in school for everyone, the greatest storyteller you ever heard. Although, Ciesiu would have to say with a bashful smile, "Sister Maxima was the greatest storyteller *after my dad.*" Ciesius' father would gather his children after supper around him (each would take turns sitting on his lap) and tell them tall tales[12] and delightful stories from his many

---

5. Max-sim-mah.
6. Kreenk-called: full of wrinkles.
7. Limp-pid: clear.
8. Pie-at-tee: holiness.
9. Prack-tick-call: useful.
10. Come-ber-sum: heavy.
11. Pue-pills: students.
12. Stories not to be believed but only to be enjoyed, like Paul Bunyan and the Blue Ox stories.

happy memories about the land of his birth, Poland. These stories, full of fun and good humor, were about Polish peasant people from the "old country" from which Ciesius' father came.

Sister Maxima's stories, however, were beautiful, inspiring religious stories. As mentioned before, her stories were about God's goodness and greatness, about God's creation of the world, sending His Son Jesus to us to give us the Church and the Holy Bible, and so on. To help children understand these sacred truths better and to remember them longer, Sister Maxima had large pictures that looked like big charts to illustrate[13] her stories.

Ciesiu was absolutely absorbed[14] in what Sister was saying, completely fascinated by the colorful pictures. He didn't realize it, but he was the most intense[15] student in Sister Maxima's class. Sometimes a child would whisper to a friend who was daydreaming or yawning in the next seat. Ciesiu was "all ears," as Sister would tell his parents and other teachers. "He doesn't miss a word I say," she would proudly report to the pastor[16] when he visited the school.

Each morning Sister would first pray with the children, praising and thanking God for the new day, for the new opportunity[17] to learn more and more about Him. Prayers were also offered for each one's family and

13. To illustrate means to show in picture form what you're talking about. In other words, the children not only heard the stories but also saw them at the same time. In those days teachers didn't have films and tapes to illustrate their teaching.
14. Ab-sor-bd: very interested.
15. In-tense: listening very closely.
16. Pass-store: chief priest of the church.
17. Op-pore-too-nit-tee: a chance to do something.

59

friends, for the sick, the poor, and the hungry. Then, as the children sat around her on little rugs (samples given by a carpet company), Sister would show one of the large, colorful pictures that she had used the day before. "Who can tell me, children," she would ask in her musical, motherly voice, with smiles, sweetness, and love, "the story that this picture illustrates?" Sometimes all hands would shoot up. At other times only some hands would be raised slowly as only a portion of the class would remember. Once in a great while as Sister held high the religious drawing or illustration, there wouldn't be a single "I know, Sister. Ask me, Sister." No hand would be visible—except Ciesiu's. "Remarkable recall," Sister would remark to herself and to other teachers later, "That child can remember names, places, details that even I sometimes forget. God has gifted him with great talent. Perhaps that little blond, chubby *boysik*[18] will grow up to be a priest." Sister Maxima did live long enough to see Ciesiu become a priest many years later.

Now, if you remember from Phyllis' story, First Holy Communion was scheduled for Palm Sunday. Like Phyllis and the rest of his classmates, Ciesiu couldn't wait for that *big day!* To receive Jesus for the first time was the greatest gift God could give to anyone, after the gifts of birth and baptism,[19] of course.

Sister Maxima also couldn't wait. She just loved to see the children so eager, ardent,[20] and innocent on their First Communion Day. Her last classroom story was about another child, a very special child who wanted more than

18. Boy-sheek: Polish-American way of saying "little boy."
19. Bap-tizm: the sacrament of becoming a Christian.
20. Ar-dent: with a very warm heart and warm feelings.

anything else to be united with Jesus in Holy
Communion. (The words "Holy Communion" mean to
be united with Jesus.)

Sister began.

"Many, many years ago (not "once upon a time" as
in fairy tales) there lived a little girl in a far away, sunny
land called Italy.[21] Her name was Imelda.[22] She loved
Jesus so much that she asked her mother and dad to let
her live in a convent[23] so that she might be able to attend
Mass with the nuns every morning and visit Jesus in the
chapel to pray to Him and His Mother Mary. She loved
her parents but also loved Jesus very much. The parents
understood as they were deeply religious[24] like their dear
little daughter.

"So Imelda got her wish.

"She was supremely[25] happy.

"But only one thing was missing. Imelda could
attend Mass each morning but was not allowed to receive
Jesus at Communion time during Mass. She was only
nine years of age. In those days (over 600 years ago,
really) you had to be at least twelve before you could
receive Holy Communion. Imelda thought she would die
before the three years were up and she would be twelve.
Time went by so slowly, as if she were riding a horse that
had leaden[26] feet.

"Now it happened one Sunday morning when she
was eleven, still one year short of her twelfth birthday,

21. It-tell-ee: country where the Holy Father, the Pope, lives.
22. Im-mell-dah.
23. Con-vent: home where nuns (Sisters) live.
24. Rill-li-jus: believing strongly in and loving God.
25. Soup-preem-lee: very.
26. Led-den: made of lead (led).

Imelda felt again that deep stirring in her heart, that deep longing to receive Jesus. Everybody in the chapel was able to approach the altar at Communion but she. How forgotten and forlorn[27] the girl felt, kneeling in her place in chapel all alone. 'Please Jesus, come to me!' was her pleading prayer.

"At that moment the priest was facing the people with the Sacred Host raised in his hand. 'Behold the Lamb of God,' he said as usual. 'Behold Him Who takes away the sins of the world.' Then, suddenly, the Sacred Host left the priest's fingers.

"The Sacred Host was now hovering[28] over Imelda's bowed head.

"Everyone gasped!

"The organ quit playing and the choir stopped singing.

"The priest stood there, startled. He looked as if he had been turned into stone. He spied the Host over Imelda's head and understood. He had seen Imelda many times in the chapel with the nuns. He knew her.

"Slowly he stirred, moved silently down the aisle, stopped before the surprised Imelda who now looked up. The priest reached for the Host and reverently placed it upon happy Imelda's tongue. 'The Body of Christ,' he whispered. Imelda replied, 'Amen,' that is, 'I believe. It is so.'

"Jesus was in Imelda.

"Imelda had just receive her First Holy Communion."

Sister Maxima's story was finished.

27. For-lorn: neglected, feeling alone.
28. Huv-er-ring: suspended in mid-air; fluttering.

The class just sat there, silent. You could hear a pin drop the silence was so great!

The children understood the story: what a great privilege it is to receive Jesus at eight years of age instead of waiting to be twelve or older.

Palm Sunday came at last—First Communion Day. All the boys were so handsome in their clean white shirts, blue ties, black shoes, and dark trousers. The girls were so pretty, all in white: white veils,[29] white dresses, even their shoes were white, patent leather white.

Four times these First Communicants marched in procession that day: first entering Church, then coming to the altar for the blest palm after the priest's homily[30] and then a little later for Jesus himself in the Sacred Host, and finally when leaving the church to be photographed, greeted, kissed, and given Communion gifts by parents, friends, the priest, and Sister.

Ciesiu would never forget his First Holy Communion. He especially remembered it when he stood in that very church at that very altar to offer his First Holy Mass as a priest sixteen years later!

Monday morning came.

The children were back in school, but only for three days as it was Holy Week, the week before Easter. Sister Maxima beamed[31] at her beloved flock[32] of innocent little lambs. One by one the children told her what happened

---

29. Vayle: head covering, usually made of cloth, worn by nuns, brides, and girls making their First Communion; also worn by women in certain countries all the time.
30. Hom-i-lee: sermon, talk given by the priest in church.
31. Beem-d: smiled broadly.
32. Flah-k: group, as of sheep or people.

in church the day before, what presents were given them, and what receptions and parties took place afterward at their homes.

Finally, it was Ciesius' turn to talk.

"Sister!" he spoke up sharply, loudly—and unhappily. "I don't want to be a tattle-tale but one girl in our class was not like Imelda you told us about!"

Sister stared.

The children stopped talking.

Ciesiu went on.

"One of the girls," lamented Ciesiu, "right after receiving Jesus, came back to her pew and instead of thanking Jesus and talking to Him, she started to clean the spots and scuff marks from her white shoes! Imagine that, Sister. Just because somebody stepped on her toes, she had to clean her shoes!"

Sister sat there, stunned.

The children sat there, stunned.

Then Sister broke the silence. For once in her life she wasn't smiling. She said in a very low and slow, sad voice: "And, Ciesiu, what were you doing watching that girl? You should have been talking to Jesus too—like Blessed Imelda!"

Ciesiu never forgot that either—even after he became a priest.

The Sparrow

Charlotte, being only eight years of age, was a child to her parents and teachers. In mind, however, she was much more mature.[1] She was a thoughtful girl for an eight year old; thoughtful in the sense that she tried to think things out. She would go over the lessons she learnt in school and the instructions her mom and dad gave her, reflecting, pondering over them wisely in her brain, trying to understand what these really meant. She was also thoughtful because she quickly came to the aid of those at home and in school as soon as she noticed someone needing a helping hand. She just noticed people's plights[2].

Charlotte especially pondered over and over again what "the Resurrection[3] of Jesus" meant when she heard that phrase in church one Sunday.

1. Mat-chure: grown-up, like an adult.
2. Plites: conditions of need.
3. Rez-zur-reck-shun: return to life.

It was Holy Week, the last week of Lent[4]. The last class before Easter was held on Monday night. The CCD[5] teachers had talked about spring and its new flowers, baby chicks hatching out of eggs, and little bunnies being born in rabbit cages, which are called "hutches." These were examples the men and women used who taught Christian children about God and the need of religion in our lives. These teachers explained that Jesus came back to life on Easter Sunday morning after dying on the cross on Good Friday afternoon nearly two thousand years ago.

Charlotte thought to herself, "How could somebody come back alive after being dead, even in springtime?" She couldn't make the connection between chicks, eggs, Easter Bunnies, balloons, chocolate rabbits, and Jesus being alive after He died.

She was still wondering what all this meant when returning home from school at the end of the week, which was Good Friday. Mother had sent her out to the front porch, which was screened against flies and mosquitoes. "It's just littered with the children's toys and other things they dropped while playing. Please tidy it up, Charlotte dear; sweep up and dust the porch furniture before coming in."

Charlotte welcomed the chore[6] as it relieved[7] her mom of further drudgery[8] and gave her more time to

4. The six weeks of special prayers, reflections, and sacrifices before Easter Sunday.
5. Catechism classes, that is, religious instructions.
6. Chor: a duty, a job to do.
7. Ree-leeved: lifted and helped, eased.
8. Drudg-er-ee: the same work, chore, job, often tiring and boring.

reflect on the topic of the Resurrection of Jesus. It was a bright, mid-April afternoon, and the sun was bathing everything in its setting shafts of glowing, golden light. Perhaps because of the brilliant sunset and the very fine wire of the porch screens, a small sparrow happily winging its way home to a nearby nest swooped by the porch and was momentarily blinded by the sun's piercing rays. It lost its bearing,[9] veered[10] sharply too soon, and struck the screen in full flight.

Charlotte cried out in pity and sympathy[11] as the little feathery creature fluttered helplessly for a few seconds, then plummeted[12] to the ground near the sidewalk by the door. It quivered[13] in pain, uttered a faint chirp, gasped, and lay crumpled in a tiny, rolled-up, brown ball of a bird.

Instinctively,[14] Charlotte rushed outside, wrung her hands in grief, then scooped the small, still sparrow to her breast, tears streaming down her cheeks. She rushed into the house with her precious prize. The tea kettle was simmering on the back burner. At once Charlotte knew what she must do. She crossed to the bathroom, plucked a face cloth off the towel rack, raced to the stove, and laid the cloth on the lid of the gurgling tea kettle. In a jiffy the cloth became, oh, so warm! With tender, loving care, the good samaritan[15] of a girl wrapped the feathery body of

9. Bear-ring: direction.
10. Veer-d: turned suddenly to the side.
11. Sym-path-ee: feelings of sorrow.
12. Plum-met-ted: dropped straight down.
13. Quiv-ver: shake.
14. In-stink-tiv-lee: doing something automatically, out of instinct, without need of much thought.
15. Sam-mare-rit-tan: the good man in the Bible who helped an injured stranger.

the bird in the hot cloth and allowed its warmth to penetrate to the very marrow[16] of its bones. Charlotte repeated this good, kind deed several times.

At her fifth try, the tiny bundle of fluff and feathers began to stir, ever so slowly! One eye, then the other, opened dazedly.[17] The right wing, followed by the left, fluttered ever so slightly. A faint heartbeat became a steady throb.[18] A cheery chirp announced it had come back to life!

Charlotte tenderly carried the birdie outside into the bright and brilliant April sunshine. She held it aloft as if offering it back to God. It shook itself as if after a bath, as all birds do, and blinked its eyes several times, as if with a satisfied smile. With a sidelong, grateful glance and another cheery peep of thanks, the sparrow suddenly spread its once wounded wings and took off. Higher and higher it soared and swooped to test its strength and then set on course for its nearby nest. Soon it was nothing more than a blur silhouetted[19] against a scarlet[20] and saffron[21] sky. Finally it disappeared amid the branches of the many trees surrounding the area.

Charlotte stood there silent and satisfied, enraptured[22] and thrilled.

She not only helped one of God's feathery creations, she at last understood what "the Resurrection"

16. Mare-row: the insides of the bone.
17. Daze-zed-lee: confused, not knowing what's going on.
18. Th-rob: beat, like a heartthrob or pulse.
19. Sill-low-wet-ted: outlined.
20. Scar-let: deep red.
21. Saf-fron: orange-red.
22. En-rapt-chured: delighted

really meant. Jesus had truly died, then as truly become alive again—not with a heated cloth, as with the sparrow, but by the power of God, by the wish of His Heavenly Father. Out of love He died. Out of love He came back to live for us.

"Alleluja!" shouted Charlotte.

Mother, upstairs, hearing the joyful acclamation[23] wondered, "What's that child up to now? It's not Easter, only Good Friday."

23. Ack-clem-may-shun: a shout of triumph and joy.

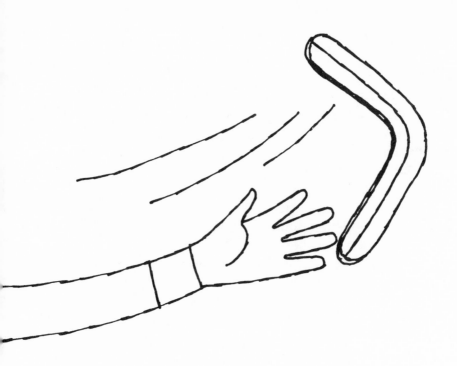

Boomerang

They lived next door to each other.

They were good friends (buddies, we say now).

Their names were James and John, like the two apostles, but everyone called them by their nicknames, Jim and Jack.

Although close companions, the two boys were different in character and personality. Jim was a happy-go-lucky fellow, full of fun and charm, always smiling and pleasant. Jack was just the opposite, surly and gloomy. Worst of all, he had the bad habit of wishing everybody bad luck. He resented anyone's good fortune,

like an "A" on the report card, a new jacket, or praise
given to another. Today we would describe Jim as
positive, outward, and open. Jack we would picture as
negative and closed to others (that is, not really caring
about people or sharing with them, except with Jim).
However, Jack once failed in being open and honest,
even with his best friend.

It happened during Holy Week, which fell that year
during spring vacation in mid-April. The two boys decided
to go walking in the woods, down in the valley below the
small town where they lived. It was a bright, balmy day,
which was welcomed after several weeks of steady rain,
"April Showers." The leaves on the forest floor didn't
crunch underfoot as they did when they were here in late
autumn, known as "Indian Summer." Everything on this
joyful April day was in bloom. Buds were breaking
through the smooth surfaces of boughs and branches on
bushes and shrubbery. Tiny berries were peeping out of
low-lying vines. Wildflowers were already in bloom in this
southern climate, gorgeous in their multi-hued spring
coats. Violets looked like a purple carpet winding between
brown and greening trees. The dainty daffodils danced in
golden garments, and crocuses bowed like floral circus
performers in their colored costumes. God's artistic brush,
it seemed, had painted Nature with every hue found in
the rainbow.

The two friends came to a small, shallow stream. It
gurgled and splashed as it raced gleefully over the stones
and stumps in its bed. The boys stopped to select some
stones from the bubbling brook. They skimmed them
across the water and listened with smiling satisfaction as
the thrown rocks plunked into the gravel bottom of the
creek. As Jack stooped to scoop up a second handful of

rocks, he noticed amid some wet leaves what appeared to be a curved stick about fifteen inches long. Jim looked, blinked, then slowly recognized what his friend had fished out of the water's edge. With a long whistle from his pursed lips he said in awe, "Jack, you just found yourself a *boomerang!*" With wonder in his eyes Jack replied, "This crooked stick a boomerang?! I wonder how it got here?" Excitedly, his blond head bobbing, Jim began to explain, "I saw a picture of a boomerang in one of our school library books. I also read a story once about a boy who made a wish, closed his eyes, and threw the boomerang as hard as he could. The boomerang came back to him, as all boomerangs do, and then his wish came true." Jack's lips curled in disdain. Instead of being glad his friend knew so much, he became instantly jealous. Without saying a word, he closed his eyes, threw the boomerang with all his might toward a clearing amid the trees, all the while saying in his mind, "I wish this smart-aleck friend of mine falls down and hits his jaw on the ground!"

No sooner had he done this when Jack himself slipped on some loose, wet stones, lost his balance, and fell. He landed on his chin, painfully cutting his jaw. The boomerang whistled by on its return flight, as expected, and struck a nearby tree, then fell clattering several yards away. Jim helped his friend to his feet. Seeing Jack's bleeding jaw, he suggested they return home at once. Holding his scratched, injured chin with one hand and clutching the boomerang in the other, Jack shuffled home behind his helpful but unsuspecting companion.

When Jack's mom saw her son's bloody jaw, she raised her voice, "Fighting, again? In Holy Week yet? Go upstairs this instant and clean off that blood! No supper for you tonight, young man! *March!*"

Jim fled the scene as explanations were useless at the moment. Dumbfounded at this unexpected turn of events, Jack stumbled up the stairs to the bathroom and sponged the blood off his face. He couldn't help think as he saw himself in the mirror how Jesus was covered with blood on the first Good Friday in Holy Week because He loved us and wished to save us. Yet he, Jack, wished his own friend bad luck! But as he pasted a Band-Aid on his cut, he began to feel a little dizzy. He padded in his stockinged feet to his room, plopped down upon his bed, and said in dismay, "What's happening here? I'm confused. Jim was to fall down, not I. Well, we will fix that!" All the thoughts he had of Jesus being covered with blood and suffering for us evaporated like steam out of a kettle of boiling water. Angry now, he made another wish. "This time," he declared, "I wish Jim gets good and sick!" He got up rather unsteadily, picked up the boomerang, and threw it as hard as he could out of the open window by his bed, shutting his eyes as he did so. The curved, flat piece of wood, which was made from the boomerang tree growing mostly in far-off Australia, swooshed through the air with a low whistle, made a wide arc around the edge of the yard, and then sailed back, hitting the house just inches from the window—and Jack's head. "It could have beaned me," thought Jack with misgivings.

Back at his home, Jim was busy helping his mom by bringing in wood for the fireplace as evenings and early mornings were still chilly. He told her what happened in the woods and how bad he felt that Jack got hurt and was scolded by his mother for something he didn't do. Jack, meanwhile, shaken at the recollection he might have been injured or the window broken by the boomerang, fell back upon his bed. His head began to ache and the dizziness returned. "Must be from hitting my chin so hard when I fell," he muttered to himself. But by nightfall, after Jack's mother felt the boy's pulse and forehead, she said kindly and with sympathy, "You have a fever, son. You better crawl under the covers. I'll forget your punishment this time and fix you a light supper. No Pepsi or pizza tonight. You're too sick."

During the night Jack got worse. The room with the nightlight on began to spin as if a merry-go-round. The doctor who lived only three houses away was summoned. He examined Jack carefully and concluded, "You'll have to stay a week in bed till the fever is spent and the infection gone."

Jack was delirious for two-and-a-half days, even though the doctor kept giving him penicillin shots and aspirin. When he came to, he weakly asked his mom to bring in his boomerang, which was still lying outside the window. He slipped it under his pillow. Then he did something he hadn't done for some time. He prayed. He prayed earnestly, not just the "Our Father" ("Lord's Prayer") and the "Hail Mary" but also in his own words, in his own way ("spontaneous" prayer). He asked God not only that he might get better in health but, more importantly, that he might improve in his behavior and attitude as well as in his relationships to others, especially towards his fine, faithful friend, Jim. Then he made his third wish. "I wish, Jesus, that Jim would get a bicycle. He doesn't have one. He's poor, you know."

That evening, Good Friday, Jack's dad came to sit upon the edge of the bed and keep the boy company for a while before attending Good Friday services at St. Nan's Church, their parish church. Jack confided to him, "Dad, I'd like a bike," without revealing that he really wished the two-wheeler for his friend, not for himself. He explained the boomerang and requested dad to pitch it out of the window with all his strength. The father shrugged his shoulders, smiled, walked to the window, and did as directed. He watched the magic stick sail away, then bank back. He ducked his head as the boomerang swished past him on its return flight and struck the side of the house, safely six feet away. He said to himself, "I'll buy the boy a bike. I can afford it. His other one is worn out. A new one would make a nice Easter present."

When dad tucked Jack in for the night before leaving, he noticed that his son's face was no longer flushed but its natural tan again. In reality, Jack felt light and comfortable for the first time since he had fallen. He drifted away into a deep, dreamless, healthy sleep.

He felt even better in the morning when dad brought him a brand-new bicycle as a present for tomorrow, Easter Sunday.

Then it was dad's turn to feel better when Jack announced, "The bike isn't for me. I want Jim to have it—as an Easter present."

Dad went out that Holy Saturday morning feeling elated indeed at his son's "resurrection to new life" (that is, at his change of attitude, at turning out to be a good Christian after all). Generously, he drove his pickup down to the shopping mall and bought another new bicycle, so that both boys could have added reason to rejoice at Easter!

In the excitement of riding away on their sleek new two-wheelers, neither boy noticed one very significant fact.

The boomerang had disappeared.

No one has ever seen it since.

No one has ever seen Jack surly or wishing anyone bad luck either.

The Easter Award

Charlotte was in her last year of high school. She studied very hard because she wanted to go to college. She also loved children and tried to help them as much as possible. That is why even though she spent many hours over her books, doing her homework, she managed to find time to be a girl scout patrol leader. Other girls her age were already dating, going to dances, and attending parties. Charlotte decided that the girls in the Flying Eagles Patrol needed her. She gave her spare time to them even though she would have enjoyed her classmates' social activities. Twice a week Charlotte would instruct each new member on how to become a tenderfoot scout, then second class, and finally a first-class scout.

Meanwhile, in her own spare moments, she was working for the highest honors in scouting. She was trying bravely to earn The Eaglet Scout Award. This required planning projects and programs and learning more and more about scouting. Already she had merit badges galore. Her left sleeve was filled with them. (In Charlotte's time sashes worn across the breast with merit badges sewed on them were not yet invented.) Her First Class Scout badge was neatly sewn on the upper right sleeve, just below the shoulder. She made a pretty picture when she wore her full scouting uniform. People turned to look at her. She regarded the color khaki nice for boy scouts, but she preferred the hunter green hue selected for girl scouts.

Now just before Christmas vacation, when the world was preparing to observe the birthday of Jesus, Charlotte was to meet with her troop leader, Miss Carol Klein. The purpose was to discuss the Eaglet Award. The appointment was for 3:30 p.m., after school in the girl scout room of Rochester High School, where the troop's various patrols held their meetings. Miss Klein was also the sophomore English teacher at Rochester High. She too felt it was important to take interest in girls of scouting age.

Charlotte appeared for her appointment punctually.[1] She was known for always being on time, which is a desirable trait[2] in everyone (actually, it is really a duty that shows respect for those whom we are to meet). Well, Charlotte waited and waited. One hour passed, then another. No Miss Klein. Deeply disappointed both at the

1. Punk-chew-a-lee: on time.
2. Tray-t: part of one's personality.

absence of the teacher and the lack of news about her coveted award, Charlotte left the now-empty school. She was dejected and on the verge of tears. No sooner had she opened the back door of her home when her mom, standing by the kitchen stove, noticed Charlotte's downcast face and weary walk. She was about to inquire anxiously what was wrong but Charlotte silently stumbled up the stairs to her room and, crushed in spirit, threw herself on her bed. Mother felt that she best wait till her daughter compose herself and tell her the bad news, whatever it was, later.

The Eaglet Award would have been a great honor not only to Charlotte but to her family as well. The Congregational Church, where Charlotte's folks worshipped, would have been the setting for the awarding of the Eaglet medal. When Charlotte came down for supper, mother said quietly, "My friend, Florence Ferrens, phoned a while ago. She mentioned in passing that the teachers at Rochester High had a pre-Christmas party this afternoon at the principal's house and then left for their Christmas vacation." Charlotte sat silent, hurt and haunted by the teacher's forgetfulness of something so important as the greatest of girl scouting achievements.

In the days that followed, Charlotte couldn't find joy in her heart on Christmas Day over anything. She did rejoice, however, that Christ was born at this time some two thousand years ago out of love for all of us. She worried and wondered too whether she would be able to enter college after graduation. Her grades were satisfactory but money was scarce. Her dad was ailing and couldn't work full-time. If he grew worse, she would have to give up her dreams of a higher education and get a job instead. As a matter of fact, she was helping out during the holidays as a stockroom clerk, putting away unsold and returned Christmas items at Mackeys, the downtown department store. She felt as dismal as the cold, gray December weather.

Then on Sunday, the day before school was to resume, the phone rang. It was Miss Klein. She was full of apologies, embarrassed and mortified that she had completely forgotten about her appointment with Charlotte. The Christmas party had caused a lapse of memory on her part. But, *good news!* "Yes, Charlotte," the teacher announced happily, "you will receive the Eaglet Award on Easter Sunday. Sorry, we thought it would be on Christmas, but I goofed by forgetting all about it."

Charlotte was in seventh heaven. Easter Sunday! What a wonderful, memorable occasion! Her sadness would be turned into joy as her dream would come true.

Easter Sunday came early that year, to Charlotte's relief. It fell on March 31st. So Charlotte's big day arrived just a bit better than three months after Christmas. She was thrilled! Many people came to church to rejoice at the Lord's Resurrection and to share with Charlotte and her family the joy of seeing such a high honor bestowed upon her. Spring too had come early and new life in Nature was already noticeable in the buds on the trees and the tulips, daffodils and crocuses peeping out of the now soft, moist earth symbolic of the grave from which the Lord rose to new life on Easter Sunday.

Charlotte looked so pretty in her freshly laundered uniform. She preferred it to the colorful new Easter outfits that many girls wore that day. How proud her parents were to see all her many merit badges that she earned with so much happy efforts over the past six years as a scout. People were also admiring her slim figure, her dusky complexion, her deep, dark, very animated and expressive eyes, her shy, modest smile, her neat bangs under her green beret.

The choir was superb in singing the glad Allelujas and Hosannas as the old organ rolled majestic chords throughout the church. After a stirring sermon on how God the Son came back to life so as to give us new and eternal life, the minister explained the second reason for rejoicing. From the pulpit he praised the girl scout movement, its leaders, members, and especially Charlotte. He was so pleased that a member of his congregation was the recipient of what every girl scout desired but only a few were able to earn—the Eaglet Award.

Charlotte was embarrassed at the unexpected praise and blushed deeply. When called to come forward to the altar for the presentation of the gold medal, her hands trembled and her knees knocked. She thought she would faint.

However, as she accepted her precious prize, she regained her composure. Invited to say a few words, she faced the admiring audience and said simply and humbly:

"It is for God and country that I worked, not for myself. I praise the Lord. He helped me achieve this honor, with the help of Miss Klein, my parents, my pastor, my friends. Happy Easter to you all."

How the people applauded!

They stood up and clapped and clapped. Miss Klein wiped a tear from her eye as Charlotte's parents and pastor hugged her. Girl scouts streamed from the pews to shake her hand; boy scouts clapped her on the shoulder.

Jesus, from heaven, smiled down on her.